Uplifting Handbook:

New Parent Edition

DANIELLE JONES

Introduction

I wrote this book with a five month old (and 13 year old) at home, while living through the difficulties of parenting a newborn. Discussing new parent struggles with friends inspired most of the contents below, I hope it buoys the spirit of other new parents.

Please enjoy it all at once, or pick it up when you're feeling discouraged and search for a particular topic.

Contents

CHAPTER ONE:

Survival Mode - I need reassurance

I can't get any sleep, it's never-ending.

Lack of sleep is the worst!! Your sleep is broken up into small bits throughout the day and you feel tired and like you're dragging around the house. Try to take care of yourself, but when you can't: be forgiving of yourself. Being exhausted is so hard, and your coping skills will be tested. If it didn't go well today, there is always tomorrow.

I can't sit down, or set down the baby, she always cries and I am so drained.

Babies rely on us for EVERY. LITTLE. THING. It's exhausting mentally, physically, emotionally. Remember that the baby won't be happy for every second of the day, it's okay to put them down (in a safe spot) to take a breather. Feeling overwhelmed is absolutely typical and you are not alone.

Feeding Baby - Breastfeeding.

It's such a challenge, I feel you.

Some days you really feel like a walking boob, living your life in 1-3 hour stretches, on and on forever. The first 6-8 weeks are the worst for pain and also second guessing yourself. Also, no one really tells you how *personal* it feels when a baby rejects your nipple. What is up with that?

After the 8 weeks you are over the hump and it starts to get easier and feel less like work, you're doing a great job and all that effort means something. It does! I see you.

Feeding Baby - Bottle & Formula Feeding:

If you tried breastfeeding and it didn't work out, I empathize. I felt like my body failed myself and my baby, and I became hyper-sensitive to others talking about breastfeeding as it brought up those defeated feelings.

However you feed your baby, they are fed and that's what matters. They will still sometimes scream and reject being fed *even when they are hungry* so in those low moments just remember that it happens to everyone and you're not messing up. You'll get through it, like you've gotten through every low moment of your life so far. You're doing awesome.

Partner Issues:

Even if you rarely had arguments with your partner prior to the baby's arrival, the emotional and hormonal lows of taking care of a young baby will introduce friction, snippiness, outbursts, etc. We are not our best selves, and our partners are not their best selves either. Your relationship is in new terrain and it's not easy or straightforward - you are both tapped out from being a caretaker.

Keep in mind that you're both struggling, aim to communicate in a productive way (avoid name-calling & be specific about what is bothering you), connect when you can, and otherwise remember that it will get better soon.

Other Relationships:

No one talks about how other relationships change! Your parents will stop asking about how *you* are doing, they just want to hear about the baby. Child-less friends may stop calling or texting. Maybe they reach out but you have no energy to get back to them. Listen - most people know that having a young baby is absolutely exhausting and they will give you a break on late replies or last-minute cancellations.

When the dust settles you can reconnect with friends and family, genuine connections make it work.

The chores are never done, my dishes aren't done and laundry is piling up. I keep "dropping the ball" with household shopping:

It's so hard knowing that you're behind on chores and there is no end in sight.

If anyone is offering to help with chores or meals, consider accepting that help!

Your number one priority right now is the basic needs of your baby and yourself. Beyond that, the dishes or the laundry can wait.

It's also so normal to "lose track" of things as a new parent, even if you're generally great about remembering them. That's a fun feature of how your brain changes as a parent! If & when this happens, keep it in context: A forgotten item at the store or being late to an appointment are (in the scheme of things) not so bad.

Am I doing this right? I don't have the motherly instinct I keep hearing about?

There's a picture in everyone's minds about the *perfect parent* who always knows what their baby needs at every moment of the day. They never forget things, always keep their cool, keep up on their hygiene, doesn't start bawling at the drop of a hat ....

That doesn't exist! When you see a Mom at the store who "has her stuff together" keep in mind she probably spent all morning getting ready to go to the store just like you - she's been spit up on just like you, and she's been cleaning poopy diapers too. Every new parent has crying moments, feelings of inadequacy, questions their own instincts, makes mistakes, and goes through it just like you.

In general, you're already doing the right things! Your anxiety & self-questioning is coming from a place of deep love and a want to be the absolute best parent you can be. Here's a secret: parents are just people, we are flawed but we can still be great parents. You will find that parenting brings out the absolute best in you, even if that's hard to see right now.

I messed up! I woke up and the baby was crying, I have no idea how long they were crying! I feel so terrible.

I'm so sorry, I know that feeling. Your body must have needed sleep so badly.

Firstly once your baby is calm, they will forget it happened pretty quickly - they are very resilient. Secondly, all we can do is move forward, we can't undo the past. What can we do to help for next time? We can make sure the baby is somewhere safe (like their crib) anytime we might fall asleep, we can ask a friend to snuggle the baby while we take a nap.

Every new parent has an experience like this, it's typical to have those heavy feelings of failure. Remember to be kind to yourself, you're only human and you're going through a lot right now.

Why haven't I bonded with my baby like I hear everyone else does? It didn't happen and I'm worried it never will. I think my baby deserves a better parent than me.

Oh no, I am so sorry. Please don't be so hard on yourself.

People bond at different paces, no matter how you came to be a parent (birth / adoption / surrogate / etc) you are the exact parent that baby was destined for, and you will bond at some point soon.

Picture in your mind a few years down the line, your child is on a big-wheel and you are walking through your neighborhood on a nice summer day, or pushing them on a swing. Picture enjoying a favourite childhood movie with them and seeing their eyes light up during a favourite scene. Picture them enjoying a favourite activity of yours (crafting, camping, cycling) and having that be "your thing".

I promise the bonding will come. Ask your partner or a friend how they think you are doing, I bet they will bring up things you've been doing that you didn't even notice. You are doing so much better than you think!

I am having a hard time accepting the new way my body looks.

Many moms and parents struggle with this. I sometimes hear people say it's part of the "magic" of Motherhood but that sounds like BS to me.

Try to not fixate on what you feel are negative, see if you can find any positives. If you aim to lose weight or gain muscle, keep realistic goals and be patient with your body.

My child is sick or hurt and I don't know what to do!

Don't Panic. You may feel responsible for their discomfort (even if it was not your fault). The first time your child gets hurt is a new painful feeling for a parent. You are still a good parent even if your child is hurt or sick, in fact they need you the most during this time. Comfort your child if needed and try to keep your focus on elements that you can control.

Will I ever have sex again?

Most new parents find they can't physically connect in the same ways, and if they could they don't have the time or the energy. Your libido and body will bounce back, but it will take time. Be patient with your partner and articulate your feelings and issues as best you can. It is not personal (even though it can feel that way), it is biological and it will improve.

My child isn't hitting a milestone and I'm concerned.

Children all develop at their own pace. Every child is different, and if you look hard you will find that your child is ahead in certain ways too. Your child is beautiful and perfect and they will get there.

CHAPTER TWO:

Affirmations - I am okay but can use a boost

You are enough.

On the hardest days, you won't feel like enough. You will feel like each little bump and hurdle is proof that you're failing. On your better days, make sure to reflect on those hard days - you will probably see that you made more progress than you realized, and any mis-steps were helping you learn a little more about your baby or about yourself.

You are doing better than you think.

If you can, I recommend any new parents to connect with other new parents. It will help your mental health and your ego to hear how everyone struggles. You'll also likely learn that there are ways that your family is succeeding where others aren't, sharing stories and support is priceless.

Don't compare yourself to other Moms or other Parents, compare yourself to where you were yesterday.

The parents you see walking their child every day in the stroller (when you can't seem to get out the door most days) seem like they've got it sorted out, but you are only seeing a snippet of their day. If you let your brain write their story (their baby behaved, happily ate, took an angelic nap, enjoyed a walk without complaint, never poops, etc) then you will never measure up.

Instead of comparing yourself to others, compare yourself to where you were yesterday, or last week, or last month. You're learning more about your baby and yourself and finding your little routines and your moments and it does get better.

Crying is Okay!

I'm not sure who needs to hear this, but crying is okay. Crying is okay and expected. It helps your body push through something difficult (or appreciate something beautiful) and that's necessary.

Venting can be positive!

Venting is different from complaining. Venting can lead to positive change. Some people (I'm sure you can identify a few in your head right now) are better to talk to because they listen with an open heart and they do not judge you or offer solutions. They just **really hear** you.

Use or find opportunities to vent. It will lighten your emotional load.

CHAPTER THREE:

Today feels pretty good, what can I do to keep positive momentum?

Catch up with family or friends.

Text or call someone to chat and catch up.

Get some sunshine.

Seize the energy you feel. Even if it's a pain in the butt, find a way to get out of the house when you are having a good day. The sunshine and fresh air will do wonders for you! Remember -if you are motivated it's difficult but do-able to get out with the baby.

Make a fun "To Do" list.

Babies can tend to make everyday tasks harder. On your good days, make a list of activities you are interested in doing with your baby (think "pumpkin patch", "go to the splash park", "sledding") this can give you something to look forward to. When you have time, pack a Go Bag with necessities and leave it by the door.

Even if it's not possible today, the next time you have a good day you can pick an activity and be out the door before you lose your motivation.

Self Care.

It's tempting to get caught up on chores when you've got time and energy, but if we *always* try to work down the chore list, we will never get to take care of ourselves in a meaningful way. Let some of the chores slide and take some time for yourself - this looks different for each person, but for me it's usually a face mask, a hot bath, loud music, a drive.

Take time outside to do something you enjoy.

This is different for each family, some may not be able to leave without the baby but some can. I encourage you to try to get outside when possible, with or without the baby. Remember to take pictures of your activity, the pictures can remind you that you're more than just your *parent side* but you also have the rest of your identity. It can help center you when you're feeling off-course.

Picture the future.

Envision yourself a few years down the line. You have settled into routines, parenting is still hard but it's not *as* hard. Your child lights up when they see you, you enjoy activities together. Friends or family compliment how good you are with your child. Your chest puffs up and you appreciate yourself for a moment, you feel capable, included, important. That future is coming.

CHAPTER FOUR:

Identity Crisis

Am I just a Parent now, or am I still all of the other roles in my life?

Right now the parenting role is front and center, but as time goes on there will be more time to reconnect with the other aspects of your life that make up your identity. Balancing parenting with work, friendships, romantic relationships, and hobbies is difficult but possible, picture the other parts on hold right now but ready to re-enter the picture.

Many parts of us change when we have a child, going out with friends will be significantly different now, it's not as simple as getting a babysitter and leaving. That being said, when you get opportunities to spend time with others please do not feel guilty for taking them. The ultimate goal is to balance, not to pour all of your time and effort into raising your children and have nothing left to put towards yourself or the other relationships you have.

Talking to people outside of your home bubble will help you reconnect to yourself. Your identity will evolve with parenthood, so you can expect to learn more about yourself as time goes on. When you take the first steps away from the house while your child is babysat, or as you feel the tug on your heartstrings when your baby smiles at you, or when a song or movie or newspaper article just hits you differently now that you have the parenthood lens.

The evolution of your identity isn't bad or good, it just is.

CHAPTER FIVE:

Final Thoughts

You are doing your best.

You are better than your worst days.

Your child loves and appreciates you (even when it doesn't seem like it).

We are all in this together.